A PR & Content Professional's Rant

Contents

Chapter 1
Internet Nirvana

Internet commerce has taken the world and particularly the West with its high Internet penetration, by storm. People are opting out of the 9 to 5 office grind; the blue collared workers are hanging up their tools, and taking to the Internet!

Not only are people outsourcing all their requirements to the least priced service or product provider, they are also ushering in a new way of life. Traffic is the holy grail of this brave world, not of the motor vehicle variety but of the type that has to do with the number of visitors to a website. People are working out of their homes-from garages, studies, perhaps from their kitchens and bathrooms as well.

There is a new kind of jargon, being used-SEO, back links, buying cycle, viral marketing, affiliate marketing, so on and so forth. There are all kinds of enticements akin to an Arabian Nights fantasy scenario, where all your desires could be pandered to, if only you followed a certain path. It is very difficult to find method in this madness.

There are interactive platforms like Upwork.com or Freelancer.com, where you can genuinely find both work and workers across a wide spectrum of industries. International payments are a breeze with enablers like Pay Pal who enable you to make and receive payments in dollars.

Then there are advisory fora like Warrior.com that let you collate collective advice on cutting- edge technology that is changing the face of Internet commerce even as we speak. There are organisations who sell software they claim directs enormous amounts of web traffic to your site, thus earning you huge pay cheques without your having to sweat for it.

You can create content, make business plans, sell electronic equipment, do truant school kids' homework or write reviews on the latest Internet games-there is really no limit to how much work you can possibly bid for on the Internet. There also scams galore, click and make money, participate in surveys and make money and things like that. Really the world of Internet commerce is very dichotomous-perplexing and liberating, fascinating and dangerous, alluring and treacherous at the same time.

Yet, there is no doubt that there is potential for making a fair amount of money. But you have to work (the key word) with the good guys and know the villains. Also the revenue model should make sense. There should be something for both or all the parties involved and there is no such thing as a free lunch. And lastly the virtual world is a great facilitator for the real world, not its replacement. At the end of the day somebody has to create the products and services that are so furiously traded on the Internet.

Chapter 2

What does PR mean to people in India?

Organised PR as an industry is of recent vintage in India, and most people have a very fuzzy idea about it. From pan chewing, safari suit wearing public sector Public Relations officers, to shady wheelers and dealers who somehow wield influence with the media to people who could sell you news space or time, much like advertising executives; there are many preconceived notions about PR as an industry.

There is no concept of PR being the science (or is it art?) of communication and advocacy-something that the legendary Philip Kotler enshrined as one of the 4 Ps (promotion, remember) of Marketing Management.

That it is a subtle, long-term and organic process which necessarily has to take a holistic approach, and is not restricted to obtaining media coverage is lost on most companies that engage the services of PR firms.

Almost always success is measured in terms of media clippings, or electronic footage a firm supplies at the end of the month. Monthly deliverables, which is exactly the wrong way to go about approaching a company's PR objectives, is usually the first thing that most prospective clients want a commitment on from their PR firms.

Frankly for most clients using PR effectively involves a learning curve. The initial days are tough with the Clients expecting coverage on demand.

"I want to figure in about half a page of that leading English daily on such and such day!"

By and by as the advocacy starts gathering momentum and the multiplier effect gathers steam, the clients come around and figure out what the whole business is about.

Just to let people have an idea about the heft of the PR function, I am going to list out its salient features

• PR strategy and planning

• Personal branding

• Reputation management

• Press Releases

• Press conferences

• Media interactions/interviews

• Site visits/tours

• CSR

• Internal communication

• Analyst and investor relations

• IPO support

• Building brand awareness

- Social media engagement

- Issues management

- Crisis communication

- Financial results and reporting

- Mergers and acquisition

- Product or service launches

- Thought Leadership

- Media briefings

- Event support

- Media training

- Editorial content: white papers, case studies, articles, newsletters, opinion pieces, etc.

Chapter 3

Impact of social media on PR

We all hear a lot about how social media is revolutionizing corporate and social communication. But is that really the case? Do we see any real and concrete evidence of that happening around us?

Or is it something that we all talk about (media agencies and corporates) and at best give perfunctory importance. What for example is the impact of social media on brand perception? How does the access to social media empower the customer? Do the various social media help increase customer loyalty?

These are metrics which need to be studied and quantified. And the important thing to remember is that one cannot approach social media randomly and hope to achieve great results. You have to plan and be very methodical.

Your messaging through these media determines the type of image you portray. So if you are given to sending out over the top messages, that is how your brand image will be perceived; so you have to be careful that whatever you put out is in absolute synergy with how you want your brand perceived.

Therefore be certain that people form the right impression. The next thing to do is to choose the right vehicles and link them to your blog. A good blog which has an interface with vehicles like Twitter, LinkedIn, Flickr, Facebook, etc. will help generate a buzz. It is important to have a consistent pattern.

A good way of communicating is to go out there and 'socialise'-for instance participate in discussions and fora that are of common interest, but always remember to control the exchange of information in a way that it adds value and does not detract from it.

Social media are in fact great in helping you connect with you target audience in a way that no other media can match. It gives you the opportunity to interact personally and directly as well as resolve problems in a better and more empathetic manner.

Social media also obtain great and honest feedback and allow you to conduct research in a more thorough fashion giving you the opportunity to give your target audience exactly the product and service they desire and not a close approximation.

Social media can enhance brand value in the most efficacious way, provided you figure out the right way of doing it. This is because no other kind of media lets you feel the pulse of your target audience, this up close and personal.

Chapter 4
Are PCs a good PR tool?

Yes if you are a showbiz celebrity, a sports or any other super star. You could also be a political heavyweight whose announcements have a bearing on the country. Otherwise the impact of most PCs (Press Conference) is zilch.

How many PCs have we slept through, where company spokespeople take you through dreary PPT presentations detailing facts about their products or services that ostensibly has no news value and therefore no chance of getting carried anywhere(in news media).

There is so much that is invested in terms of time, effort and money in PCs, that one really needs to take a serious look at the whole concept. PR agencies recognise this and if they agree to holding a PC, they do so with the proviso that there be bankable celebrities present, whose pictures or footage could then be presented as coverage, even though it might not at all add value to the brand or even detract from it.

If for example a multinational had decided to set up shop in India, and they decide to call a Bollywood A- lister for the launch PC, all the news would be about the impending release of that person's next big budget movie, rather than the nitty gritty of the business model the company has in mind for India.

There are of course press conferences that are hugely successful and impactful. These usually have to do with momentous occasions. Like India signing the nuclear deal with the United States, or Apple launching its next product (that is momentous).

Or you have Tom Cruise make his maiden trip to India (that is momentous for his fans). Alternatively it could be about dramatic or salacious revelations that appeal to vicarious sensibilities of lay readers (a closet homosexual celebrity coming out in the open).

The bottom line is that press conferences are useful if they are warranted. If there are reporters clamouring for information about your company's activities it is a good idea to collect them at one place and disseminate the information in an organised manner. For example if a hospital has been getting negative press consistently, and the hospital administration wants to set the record straight and give their side of the picture; then a press conference is just the thing to go for.

A stage-managed or contrived press conference may get you some manner of coverage, but it will not do much good to the image of the company or organisation in the long run. It is far better to engage the media organically over a length of time, and get them to know your products, services or cause for what it is, and let them carry forward the message at the right time.

Chapter 5
Why CSR is a must for Indian companies irrespective of size

First the moral reason. Despite India being among the fastest growing economies of the world, and the world singing hosannas to the emerging Indian middle class, it scores extremely poorly on most human development indices. The arrival of the FI Grand Prix (which has since departed) and the fact that India now has a booming automobile industry cannot mask the co-existing abysmal poverty that is all too evident.

Poverty is not an invisible underbelly in India. It is up front and stark, but we all pretend that we don't see it. Much as the British colonialists went to their clubs, gymkhanas and golf courses in pre-independence India, not caring to notice the plight of the common Indian who lived an emaciated existence, much of middle class India which is the backbone of the new corporate sector is blind to the misery of their fellow Indians.

This does not reflect well upon us as a people. Where is our moral conscience? How can we be so insensitive to our fellow human beings? The second and perhaps decisive reason is self-interest.

The present economic development model is not tenable. It will lead to tremendous unrest. You have to make everybody join in the good times. Look at the sheer numbers of the deprived. How long will they silently watch as the privileged amongst us live better and bigger than ever before?

Now more than ever before we need everybody in the fold. The benefits that will accrue will be tremendous. As we help marginalized people join the mainstream, they will eventually become economic force multipliers. They will lead to economic activity of a scale that will be global in its ramifications.

The government is doing what it can to help. The private sector has to pitch in- in our cities, towns, villages, and tribal area. It has to build schools, plant trees, help with rain water harvesting, clothe and feed the poor, distribute books-there is so much that can be done in India.

It is heartening to see that companies in the corporate sector are now joining hands with the government and NGOs and helping with community development, environment issues, besides pure philanthropy. This needs to continue and be taken to the next level. We need our Andrew Carnegies, Warren Buffets, Bill Gates and Rockefellers. The smaller companies have to get their act together so that CSR is given the prime importance that is due to it.

The media professionals have to pitch in by providing adequate coverage to all manner of CSR activity. PR and advertising plans should always have a CSR component, as the easiest thing to do in India is social activity. There is so much that is wrong. From uncovered drains to dirty toilets, from streets without lighting to classrooms without books-there are so many causes that can be taken up.

Let CSR be the number one priority for the next decade and see how India moves up the human development indices. Only then will we be able to hold our own on the world stage. All the pretty people in the world driving around in their Ferraris won't do it for us. It is our masses who will do it for us. But they have to be clothed and fed first.

Chapter 6

Impact of commercialization of news on the PR profession

Traditionally PR has always been viewed with some suspicion. The image which a PR person carried until not very long ago, at least in India was that of a sort of a fixer, a member of the dirty tricks department, somebody you used to resort to subvert the media, and worse bribe them to toe your line or sing your tune.

It is only recently especially in the last ten years so that PR professionals have been recognised for what they are-practitioners of the discipline of advocacy- that uses effective and calibrated communication to convey the best image of one's clients through media and non-media vehicles.

The rise of the PR profession in India coincided with a tremendous media explosion. From a state run television broadcaster and a few legendary newspapers the country saw the entry of scores of round-the-clock TV channels, and hundreds of newspapers and magazines from across regions.

While this definitely benefited the consumer of content, who witnessed a veritable information revolution they could not even have imagined, just a few years before, the quality of content was sometimes the casualty.

This was because of the inevitable shake-out in this fast growing industry. Bottom-lines began to dominate; paid news made its entry, and indeed became mainstream-thanks in no small measure to the respectability accorded to it by the nation's premier newspaper house.

How does this augur for the PR industry? Ironically not very well at all, contrary to what one might imagine. PR builds its equity on the fact that it advocates and does not hard sell. It conveys news about something; does not advertise a message.

By implication there is no exchange of money or consideration. All the money that gets paid is the retainer at the beginning of the month to the agency for its professional expertise. Now if all news could be bought and not pitched, nobody would employ the services of a PR professional; they would all go to advertising agencies instead. And news itself would not remain news for very long.

Everybody knows an advertorial when they see one. No matter how you dress up paid news, if you are going to name brands in the grossest possible way, and pay lip service to the industry under review, you are harming the brand equity of both the product and the newspaper. This cannot go on indefinitely.

There will be a time when highly respected newspapers would have turned into trade directories-who would like to read a sublime editorial in a trade directory? A bit alarmist, perhaps?

My point is that as much as the newspaper industry or the community of journalists, PR professionals too would like the news media to move away from gross commercialisation.

Chapter 7

Digital PR in India

Is there really such a thing as organised digital PR in India? Worldwide digital PR is credited with creating huge success stories for corporations, professionals and individuals. This has a lot to do with the fact that in the developed markets of the world, the online universe is truly understood for what it is- a seamless, precise and highly calibrated means of communication.

In India in spite of the huge evidence of its cost effectiveness and efficiency there seems to be an inertia which dogs the use and application of this highly effective means both by communication consultants and their clients. This is not to say that many Indian companies do not aggressively use digital PR or that there aren't communication professionals who specialise in it.

But it is nowhere as important or pervasive as it should be. Consider this. Facebook at last count had 195.2 million MAUs or Monthly Active Users in India and this number is growing. Which mainline newspaper can boast of this kind of highly focused as well as segmented reach?

This is a goldmine sitting to be tapped. How many PR consultants and Corporate Communications heads devote the kind of time they should to optimally utilise Facebook's phenomenal reach.

Inherent to digital PR are certain advantages that it offers over its traditional counterpart. First and foremost the shelf-life of the messaging is considerably longer than in traditional media. Secondly the messaging is interactive, which lets you instantly gauge response.

What's more you could then go ahead and integrate it with social media tools. Digital PR in fact has the wherewithal to directly accrue revenue/attention to your client, by in a sense creating a direct hotline (to borrow a term from older times) with the target audience. What's fantastic of digital media coverage is the fact that you can track its reach quite easily and precisely and know how exactly it's faring.

A lot of resistance to digital PR arises from the fear of the unknown- the fact that it deploys technology. This is actually typical of any period that witnesses a paradigm shift in the way things are being done. The world is going digital and a lot of us are not quite comfortable with the fact. Why there are still people in India and even in the West who cannot send text messages. So it is not surprising that the real power of digital PR is yet to be effectively harnessed.

Chapter 8

PR- The Way Forward.

The PR industry in India is increasingly gaining acceptance with a greater understanding of what it entails amongst not just the large companies, but across businesses of all sizes and scale. The clientele ranges from mighty corporate firms to tech start- ups to budding artists to politicians to what have you.

The reason for this is that PR provides a far bigger bang for the buck than any other form of communication and everybody who has realised this wants a piece of the action. However, PR firms today operate in an ever changing media scenario, where newer forms of communication like social media and the concomitant churning in the traditional media have compelled a re-think on traditional PR strategy.

In order to remain relevant PR firms in India need to constantly innovate so as to be able to keep pace with the latest developments and changes both in their media and non-media based approaches. PR firms today have to demonstrably be able to prove the efficacy of their craft. Broadly they need to increasingly focus on the following:

1. Quality Content: At a time when there is an abundance of PR firms and consultants, what will distinguish one from the other is the ability to create quality content that is contemporary and effective.

The days of the ubiquitous press release are over. Content creation is specialist business and one needs to have the skills to leverage it equally well to both traditional and social media. Equally important is the ability to reach out to a non-media audience of influencers, and indeed the target customers of the client directly.

2. Quantifying Results: Traditionally PR firms would quantify their performance by measuring the total media coverage (space or time) in terms of ad rates and multiply it by a further factor ranging from 2 to 5. This often left the clients dissatisfied as they had no way to accurately find out the impact it had in terms of consumer response.

However the increasing role of Digital PR has made quantifying pretty straight forward. You know how many and what type of people have accessed the content and what they think of it.

In times to come Digital PR is going to drive communications campaigns and the fact that this form of PR can show you where the money is, makes it a very powerful tool indeed. You will be able to study the data, extrapolate it and predict a highly effective course of action for the future.

3. Focus: Worldwide (including India) there is a tough economic environment with firms and companies looking to save the last dollar or rupee.

In such a scenario PR firms and consultants should be able to take a focused and calibrated view of the client's objectives and come up with plans that show visible results. Media and other exposure should result in leads, sales and expansion for the client. The bottom line is the bottom line.

Chapter 9

Does the economy look okay?

When you look around yourself do you get the sense that you live in a BRICS economy that is attracting all the capital in the world and where people are enthralled at the prospect of many years of growth or do you feel a sense of despondency around you? You really can't tell, can you?

The mega scams of the recent past, the cynical electoral deals that the political parties make, and the fluctuating value of the rupee don't let you decide, one way or the other, do they? Yet the good times too don't end either. Car makers keep on announcing new models. People are still buying their second or third homes.

Eating out has not diminished, and despite the hike in airfares, people are travelling more than before. At the same time we all do find the going tough in our jobs and our businesses. Orders come after a struggle, every penny is fought over. Clients cancel or renegotiate contracts and the payments take their time in coming in.

Fuel prices do a yo-yo dance; food inflation has been high for far too long now (come down since demonetization) with things like fruits priced, almost beyond the reach of the common man. The Indian middle and upper middle classes are holding on to their recently acquired affluence (tennis clubs and swimming pools in gated housing community projects) by somehow hanging in there.

The poor and the underprivileged (as also the lower middle class) must be growing through harrowing times with respect to the price of food items. While in many sectors like housing and infrastructure there is a noticeable slowdown, one sees a veritable explosion in the health and education sectors, with international tie-ups, bench-marks and affiliations being bandied about with gay abandon by every trader and builder who has entered the fray- beware Ivy League, here come the best universities in the world. Viva Ghaziabad, Noida, Faridabad, Jalandhar and perhaps Meerut! What happens to the poor students once they pass out is anybody's guess.

India is a young country in terms of its demographic profile. With a huge market like this where the majority of the people are in the earning age-group, everybody in the world wants a finger in the pie. Never mind things like the suitability of the products and services to the market.

But all the same any investment and economic activity does create jobs and there is development no matter how lop-sided. So how does the citizen of this country feel? Where Jaguar and Jugad (locally assembled auto-motive contraptions), Lear jets and bullock-carts (still find them not far from any urban centre), call-centres and manual scavenging, computers and medieval mind-sets all compete for attention.

Do they feel that the economy is rocking? Or are they as clueless as you and I?

Chapter 10
PR in times of slowdown

At the best of times PR is a misunderstood profession in India. It is viewed upon something like a dirty tricks department rather than an organised and professional part of the marketing plan of a company.

Even the so called corporate organisations, who should know better evaluate a PR firm or a consultant's success in terms of the amount of media coverage they will manage to obtain. So at the time of interviewing a prospective agency, there are questions about the size of coverage and the pedigree of the publications and TV channels. Why not buy ads then?

PR consultants too get caught up in this insidious game, and come up with their own set of preconditions for obtaining such coverage. If you remember your economics lessons from school, for every theory there would be a set of preconditions often couched in the words, "other things remaining the same".

Likewise PR consultants try to ensure any shortfall in promised coverage is attributed to the neglect of certain preconditions. This leads to a sort of an adversarial client-consultant relationship where the former tries to see how much print space or time they are able to wring out, and the latter are focused on trying to increase the number of news items that appear, irrespective of whether it is in the best interest of the client.

When times are rough for most businesses, PR and advertising agencies often get the rough end of the stick when it comes to receiving payments. Delays are endemic and quite often full payments are never made.

This leads to agencies insisting on advances, which in turn results in loss of business. The worst casualty of the whole process is that something as vital as advocacy and organic promotion, especially in economically stressful times does not receive the due attention it deserves.

Instead of getting fixated on something as abstract as coverage both marketers and PR consultants need to wake up and smell the coffee and realise that there is something called a digital universe, which is completely and totally ROI driven and accounts for every single penny spent. There is no scope for vague and unrealistic expectations here.

Businesses worldwide are beginning to realize that this is the way they can get a huge bang out of every buck spent and in a minutely calibrated fashion too. PR consultants need to upgrade their Internet marketing skills and understand the nuances of this game.

You don't just issue a press release to a mainline newspaper or even to an online news portal any more. You need to go to authority bloggers. Your online press release is no good if it doesn't have back links. What sort of online reputation do the client and indeed the PR consultant have?

Top drawer professionalism and familiarity with cutting-edge technology is the only way forward in the times ahead.

As Internet penetration gains even more traction both businesses and PR agencies need to upgrade their skills and leverage the immense possibilities. The time to squabble over traditional media coverage may soon be over.

Chapter 11

Learning Advocacy

Blowing your own trumpet or beating your own drum will not win you many fans. But having someone else advocate your cause will leave people intrigued. This is what lies at the heart of PR, but alas this basic fact is often forgotten in the day to day machinations that clients and PR consultants alike pass on as Public Relations.

Advocacy lies at the very heart of professional and ethical PR, and the more we veer away from this basic tenet, the more harm we cause to the cause. Like it or not the origin of PR is shrouded in murky propaganda deployed by early twentieth century governments and industrialists of North America in pushing their agenda.

By and by as PR as a profession moved towards respectability, it came to be realised that for it to be seriously considered as an agent of public good, it had to operate by a set of ethics.

While it advocated the cause of its clients, it should do so by way of representing and communicating the facts in a manner that was above board and truthful.

This in essence meant that the interests of the intended recipients of the message were recognized as being equivalent with those on whose behalf the message has been crafted.

The difference between advocacy and propaganda is the difference between a democracy and a dictatorship. In a democracy you have the right to free speech. This means that you are free to publicly advocate any cause, as long as you convey facts and do not resort to lies or slander.

You are at liberty to interpret and apply perspective, and people have the right to accept it or reject it. How successful you are depends upon the facts of what you are advocating and how skilfully you can represent them.

In the case of a dictatorship the messaging is controlled and force-fed. Neither do the recipients have access to any other source of information, nor are they allowed to express their doubts or displeasure.

If the North Korean people are told that birds cried and the weather changed when their beloved leader died and if any of them disbelieved that fact they would be shot, the message would go across! But it would do the people no good. In the former case everyone is equally free to advocate, in the process enabling the people to make the best choice.

PR consultants, who understand advocacy for what it is, know that the groundswell created by it will far outlast the results obtained from the most expensive advertising campaign in the world. This is because unlike advertising which builds hype, advocacy builds goodwill.

When Obama launched his first presidential campaign, even his most ardent supporter would have baulked at the odds against him. But his articulation of an alternative vision and template of growth caught the fancy of an America which was in the throes of transformation.

People were sick of the excesses of the past, and tired of the bad news about a floundering economy and unending foreign wars. So much so that people voted him into office a second time.

Advocacy by its very nature requires time to fructify, and this is something that both clients and PR consultants need to know right at the start. But the payback is well worth the wait.

Chapter 12

Why harp about content?

Everyone has been harping about the importance of content for a very long time now. So much so that it is beginning to sound clichéd. Why then do marketing experts swear by content? Well apparently they have genuine reasons for plugging content.

When was the last time you paid enough attention to a product being advertised on TV, to want to go ahead and buy it? Do you care to go through all the email messages you have a subscription for? You would probably not even look at direct mail.

If an overwhelming majority of marketers both to the direct consumers and other business marketers use content to sell their products and services, it is because they get tremendous bang for every buck they spend.

Customers take to content quite easily and willingly as it is friendly, personal, highly informative and most importantly interactive. Brands realize this to the extent that many of them have become publishers of content.

In fact traditional publishers are taking a leaf out of content marketing and digitizing their content platforms in order to survive and thrive in the new dispensation.

In spite of the overwhelming evidence supporting the

efficacy of content marketing and a lot of noise about it, the majority of businesses don't have an efficient and structured content marketing strategy in place.

This may be out of inertia, perceived lack of time or a lack of appreciation of its benefits. However the business strategists of most companies only need to think about the sheer lost opportunity in their delaying the adoption of content marketing as an integral part of their marketing strategy going forward.

 The horse drawn carriage continued to be around much after the first motor car was invented. But it was only after everyone moved on to this new mode of transportation that the modern era truly began.

The inexorable expansion of the Internet and people's increasing engagement with it make it the best platform for intimately communicating with one's target audience. The ones who seize the opportunity and invest in a viable content marketing strategy will certainly have a head start over those who dilly dally.

One should also bear in mind the fact that content marketing thrives on genuine content creation and not gimmickry. Its impact is organic and felt over time. Some of the biggest brands in the world realize this and take their content very seriously indeed. Sooner or later any business worth its while will have to do that to stay relevant.

Chapter 13

The perils of being a Public Relations professional in India

It is not easy to be a Public Relations professional in India. From being completely misunderstood as a profession to little or no appreciation of its tremendous importance to corporations and organisations, Public Relations as a professional service has not received its due at all.

This is quite unlike advertising and event management which are willy nilly recognized as bona fide professional industries. In public perception Public Relations is equivalent to the dirty tricks departments of corporations, which somehow tries to pass on laudatory but half-baked and often exaggerated information pertaining to their clients to a gullible press.

Nothing could be farther from the truth. PR professionals will not pass on any information that will not make sense, or is likely to be laughed off by an intrinsically and rightly sceptical Indian media.

Far from eating out of the hands of PR professionals as the world and sometimes the clients (who ought to know better) believe, journalists will not pick up even those stories which are obviously news worthy, for the simple reason, that they never have a dearth of news worthy stories.

If a competent PR professional does have a way with certain journalists, and is able to get his or her story published, it most likely has to be the result of them having done their homework in terms of facts and research right, every time they pitch a story. This creates a bond of trust between the journalist and the PR representative. No serious PR practitioner will let anything spoil this symbiotic, but strictly professional relationship.

That is why it is critical that a PR professional choose his or her clients with care. Pedigree and integrity have to be the watchword here. You would put a years' old carefully built up relationship with senior journalists at risk if your clients weren't up to much good and you had to represent them.

Of course for you to get those kinds of clients you need to have the commensurate skill set- excellent communication ability, a fair understanding of matters pertaining to business, and the capability of pitching relevant stories to the media.

In a far from perfect world, you will of course come across clients who are megalomaniacs and patently unreasonable, PR representatives who are totally at sea about what is expected of them, and moronic journalists with the IQs of kindergarten children.

As a PR person you need to be able to quickly identify the kind of clients you could develop a working relationship with, and the kind of journalists you can have an equal and mutually satisfying professional relationship with.

But by far the most challenging part of a PR representative's job has to be the safeguarding of their commercial interests. Most clients tend to overlook the fact that positive news coverage is worth its weight in gold, and counts for much more than an exorbitantly priced ad. You pay for an ad. and it gets published. There is no intellectualising and pitching involved. Besides most people don't believe what comes in ads.

Do you get gratitude or gratefulness for news coverage you helped them get from the client? More of often than not there is quibbling about the size (*kitne sq cm hai*?), and how their product or service was bound to be covered by the press!

What's more, instances of clients not paying, or paying in part abound. That is why insisting on advance payments is always a wise option.

Chapter 14
Marketing Communication in the Days Ahead

For many years now we have been hearing that traditional advertising is not the way of the future, and of late we hear that the advent of paid news will make traditional PR untenable soon, and the only way ahead is online communication and all that it entails-emails, blogs, articles, social media posts, online video, webinars, and anything else IT comes up with.

Is it really true? Are we completely and irrevocably going to move away from the familiar comfort of dispatching information through good old newspapers, television, radio, magazines et al?

In India where the newspaper industry continues to grow on the back of many more millions emerging from poverty and being able to buy and read newspapers, albeit the vernacular ones, such a scenario seems very unlikely for a long time to come.

The similar growth and decentralization of television channels in different parts of the country would also point to the continuing growth and relevance of traditional media. This is however contrary to the trend in the western world where traditional media seem to be increasingly struggling to keep pace with the onslaught of modern online media-exemplified by the purchase of The Washington Post by Jeff Bezos, founder and CEO of Amazon.

The importance of online communication is undoubtedly far more pronounced over there with   ever expanding budgets being allocated for effectively leveraging the medium, which is becoming increasingly sophisticated and complex.

India is woefully inadequate in terms of Internet connectivity with a mere 34.8% of the population having access; but in terms of sheer numbers at 462 million users it is at a highly impressive number three worldwide.

In terms of their purchasing power these Indian netizens pack an almighty punch, forming as they do the crème de la crème of the Indian society, whose spending patterns fully replicate those of their Western counterparts. It follows therefore that online communication has increasingly become an important component of any marketing strategy.

What promises to be a game-changer in online communications in India however is the emergence of smart mobile phones as a platform for receiving the Internet. With a gargantuan mobile phone subscriber base of 1 billion, the possibilities for Internet commerce are immense.

Already mobile handset manufacturers and mobile telephone service providers have respectively started creating cheaper smart phones and subscription plans to tap into these colossal numbers. The advantages of using online media over the traditional forms of media are clear and obvious.

From costing a fraction of what the use of traditional media entails, to a more intimate interaction with the target audience by way of direct feedback and the possibility of exact measurement of impact created, online media wins hands down on all important markers of efficiency and effectiveness.

So notwithstanding the parallel growth of traditional media on account of demographic changes in India's vast interiors, online communications is going to lead the charge in reaching out to people in a more direct and effective way. With mass scale Internet connectivity through mobile phones promising to change the landscape and demographics of Internet usage in India we seem to be sitting on the cusp of an e-commerce revolution.

Chapter 15

The Changing Face of PR

The face of the PR industry is changing at a rapid pace, even without many of the people who are a part of the industry and should know better, realizing it. The landscape that is evolving is increasingly dominated by digital media, and those that are unable to discern in which direction the wind is blowing will eventually fall by the wayside.

Quick results are expected in an era where social media get the news out way faster than traditional media platforms. As a result traditional media outlets are metamorphosing into digital news platforms, putting out news content on their websites, which is shaped by the expectations of a social media savvy target audience.

There is no denying the fact that the younger lot joining the PR workforce has a more instinctive and organic relationship with technology and are able to understand its nuances and can leverage its power far more effectively than their seniors.

It is for the latter to pick up a few tricks on how to do that and thereby learn to use technology in a way that enhances one's ability to outreach, profess and obtain effective consumer attention(not media attention), like never before.

In these changed circumstances the PR agency model as we knew it will probably change dramatically from the way that it is structured right now. There is already a perceptible shift underway in the nature of PR agencies.

More and more PR outfits are smaller and specialised outfits that are better able to meet the quick turnaround expectations of their clients. It may not be the case today that PR firms that pay lip sympathy to tools like blogging, social networking profiles and online video, and so on, will fold up, but they will surely one day- as surely as the email enervated snail mail. The writing is on the wall, and PR professionals ignore it at their own peril.

As time marches by, one will see a decline in influence of traditional journalists and opinion influencing analysts and the rise and rise of the power of the blog. This is not surprising in a scenario, where three new blogs are being created every two seconds!

Brands now have to receive inputs and evolve and not attempt to bring the consumers to speed as was the case in the past. The best way to find out about the reputation of a brand is not by referring to all the ads, newspaper and television coverage one has garnered, but the rank it obtains in an online search. It's time for the PR thinking heads to change tack or other specialists will take over.

Chapter 16

Grappling with Tech PR

Tech PR is the future. All PR professionals know it and have apparently been gearing up for it. Everyone wants to know what the new-age PR techniques are and how those can be effectively leveraged on behalf of clients. How does one use social media and mobile communications to put individuals and companies in a position of being instantly able to connect with their target audience in an intimate and interactive manner?

Driving this change in the way that PR and Communications are being conducted is the inexorable migration of traditional media to the online platform. At the same time there is the growing influence of the hitherto ignored bloggers and even podcasters.

While using technology has enormously benefited all PR professionals-after all one can easily send a press release to thousands of journalists at one go, it also has its own pitfalls to deal with. Journalists are more likely to dismiss this sea of press releases as spam and reject even genuinely meritorious stories.

However the area where most traditional PR practitioners find themselves at a tremendous disadvantage is in addressing the Internet generation who source all their information online and inherently resent being instructed in a heavy handed fashion in their social media dominated world.

They are most likely to take an opinion from bloggers and contemporaries on social media. One is required to join the community when it comes to this set and learn to talk their lingo in all honesty.

At the same time as web and mobile technology continue to rapidly evolve, newer digital PR strategies have to keep apace. Perfecting social media and mobile outreach requires for content to be appropriately optimized.

Skills increasingly will involve the right insight, technology and creativity abilities. Increasingly the trend is for small PR firms to partner with companies, especially start-ups and stay the course right through the product life cycle of the products or services in question.

The organic nature of how technology PR helps products connect in an evolutionary manner make this possible. While all this goes on there will be increased scrutiny of the level of privacy maintained by PR firms that handle large volumes of data.

With e-commerce becoming an integral part of most companies' marketing strategy, tech PR will see a burgeoning of demand for its services and expertise, with the spotlight on social and visual media. There are in fact going to be ever new imaginative ways of reaching out to one's focused target audience, and the PR companies who get their act together and master these techniques first will get a first mover advantage.

Chapter 17

Content Rules and Rules

The time for content has come and how. Press Releases though not yet passé, don't catch enough attention. High quality cutting edge content is the new mantra to engage one's traffic audience. Can't get that to them, you are in big trouble. Period.

But the reality is that content as a means of pitching your products and services is not new or novel concept. Most companies have been using content in the shape of blogs, reports, surveys, news-letters et al for a number of years. Only they didn't know that what they were doing was creating content.

However it is in the sharply focused leveraging of content as a means to expand one's product or service footprint by way of holistic brand building and more efficient lead generation that one has moved away from the traditional methods of positioning content as an effective marketing implement.

This requires for organizations to get their acts together in the areas of both editorial and marketing. Among other things, it requires a firm handle on the PR, SEO and social media aspects of one's outreach strategy.

More than anything, including making prolific PR the mainstay of one's strategy, one needs to focus on quality. With a multiplicity of media channels, including the all-pervasive social media, available to marketers and advertises, the emphasis of this cannot be overstated.

This is on account of the fact that the target audience now has the wherewithal to provide feedback that you need to respond to. You put out inane marketing drivel, they will just disconnect.

People are no longer going to lap up anything you dish out. They will respond if you are talking to them about something that addresses their concerns. Lastly you will eventually run out of marketing spiel to hand out.

You really do need to work very hard on the content that you advocate, or it won't work for you. Just updating your posts or getting out press release after press release amounts to little more than some pompous spamming.

In order for your content to be able to set the social media space on fire, it needs to be useful, entertaining and catchy. If it is not, then you are either not enhancing your online prestige or are busy downgrading it.

Chapter 18

Famous online better than famous offline

Most people in the Western world and large sections in the rest of the world have a real life persona and an online persona. This is especially true of young people, also known as the Internet generation.

Almost everybody these days communicates by email, rather than rely on the good old postal services. Texting and video chatting have become mainstream and e-commerce has willy nilly entered all our lives.

Don't we remit money or receive it into our bank accounts online, and haven't we all used the credit card to make purchases online? We all swear by eBay for God's sake!

The point that one is trying to make here is that we have a very active online life that co-exists with our offline life. But a debate really arises when we have to choose between performing the same function in the traditional or off line fashion or the contemporary online way.

Take the case of making payments. You have the option of writing a cheque or making an online transfer. Cheques are relatively safer, but can't match the speed or convenience of an online money transfer.

Another example is socialising. Communicating via the net obliterates distance and time differences, but if you want to enjoy a coffee together with your friend or watch the sunset together, you have to do it offline. But the wonderful thing is that as online technology evolves we may be able to even do things that we right now consider impossible- like smelling coffee. The coming days will see the Online vs. Off line debate getting more and more interesting.

What makes online-famous a different kettle of fish? Now you might turn around and say that to me it does not matter that I got famous the old fashioned way, without having to use the Internet, and what ultimately matters is the result. You may be right and you may be wrong.

While it is true that one can get famous using traditional media like TV, newspapers and magazines, one cannot claim that these media represent you and what you have comprehensively. Getting famous using the Internet on the other hand lets your target audience know you and what you stand for more intimately.

They can personally connect with you on your blog, and you can chat up with them as frequently as you want. You can use analytical tools that will let you know precisely who is interested in your offering and how many of those are establishing contact.

The thing about being spotted on the Internet is that it is a very democratic and a cheap as well as fair process where everybody gets a shot at being successful, whereas in the traditional model you need to knows how to work the levers of the system for things to really work for you.

Look at this in another manner. In the old days one relied on one's family, community, society and religion to get along in life.

At that time one needed that support. As time went along and technology reduced our dependence on people, one's number of friends and acquaintances dropped dramatically.

In the modern era, the time immediately preceding the Internet saw most people having about three people they counted as friends. This was perfectly fine except that you could not use the three to spread the word about say the new book you wrote. You would have to pay professionals to do that.

With the advent of Internet all of that has changed. The average person has more than a hundred friends on the various social networking sites and these are a valuable resource in case you want the word spread about something.

Word can spread like a viral infection on the Internet and make a mega celebrity out of a nobody in a matter of two or three days. This even has a term-viral marketing. So you see the Internet has changed the rules of the game completely and the goal-posts have been moved a lot closer for everyone's convenience.

Be known online

The online world has assumed a huge amount of significance in today's times and this is only going to grow and grow. It would therefore stand you in very good stead to mark your presence in it in a very telling way. You simply have to develop your social presence in a manner that you are effectively able to leverage your attributes, skills, likes and dislikes to a vast and appropriate audience.

Social networking sites led by Facebook and Twitter are fast and ruthlessly efficient enablers of this- far more effective than traditional media like newspapers and television, and best of all cheaply available and accessible to everyone. Today the youth are defining and constantly re-shaping and evolving the digital world by their socialising, entertaining, learning and studying and following the latest trends online.

You are not a part of it, you might as well as not exist (at least digitally). Period.In order to be heard you have to be on top of the game. E-mail and Instant Messaging are baby steps in this world. You have to be part of online communities where you contribute actively and constantly interact while at the same time learning to innovate.

Be it blogging, web-casting, trending, on-line trading-your transactions will build up for you an online profile by which people will gauge you. Much like in the world of finance, each country or for that matter each individual has a credit rating, so it is in the world of the Internet. You have to make your presence felt.

The power of the Internet as a harbinger of change was brought home by the highly effective way in which Arab youth were able to harness its power to bring about The Arab Spring. This was something the previous generations could not achieve, as they did not have the tremendous power of the Internet at their disposal.

We are in the throes of the mighty digital revolution and the youth are the ones who are driving it and it is in their individual interest to put their individual stamp on it.

Uninterrupted Economic Success

The Internet is a medium that can be effectively used to achieve overnight success. Now whether this success is a flash in the pan or sustainable over a long period of time depends upon how you play the game.

Overnight success does not come to many and the lucky few who get it might have worked really hard to achieve it or might have been plain lucky, but what is important is how they manage it, or whether they are able to sustain it or indeed grow it.

The Internet not only empowers the individual but by extension the community, the nation and finally the world. In countries like India for example with every passing year Internet penetration increases and with it increases the opportunity for the Indian youth who have already gained a formidable reputation for their IT prowess, to make India the crucible of new ideas and innovation.

This has the potential to pitchfork the Indian nation way ahead of where it is now quite rapidly and truly become the world's economic power house. India with its democracy, rule of law and well established institutions patterned after those of the West is perhaps better equipped to achieve this than an at present richer, but dictatorial China, which denies its citizens the freedom to think freely and therefore innovate, a prerequisite in this bold new world of the

Internet with its ever evolving and changing by the minute paradigm.

Truly living the Internet life will be the ultimate game changer for mankind and we are in the throes of a lifestyle metamorphosis which is of no less significance than the momentous occasion millions of years ago when man first learnt to walk upright. Nothing is going to be the same again.

Chapter 19

Young Internet Millionaires Harnessing the Power of the Web

New Age Entrepreneurship

We have all heard stories about obscure teenagers turning into huge celebrities overnight. They are children who, by the time they came into their teens turned their everyday hobbies and passions into multi-million dollar enterprises; all by reaching out to vast numbers of like-minded individuals on the Internet.

Before we begin to understand what it takes to bring about these tremendous transformations, let us begin by going ahead of us and taking a sneak preview into what sort of lifestyle changes a (formerly) regular person experiences, as a result of becoming an online celebrity.

Somebody like Mark Zuckerberg, the billionaire founder of Facebook cannot step out onto the street without attracting a crowd of photographers, journalists, tourists, autograph hunters and possibly a posse of policemen for their security.

You become an internet millionaire at a young age and the world is your oyster. The best cars, snazzy mansions, incredible holidays, and the best people to date-you will get all that and more.

If you are really at the top of the heap every newspaper and magazine, worth their salt, would like to feature you, and there will be offers to write books (perhaps your autobiography which can be turned into a book). Large multinational corporations would like to sign business deals with you and you will be a youth icon and role model for the young of the world.

Successful Online

There are a number of people who have made a mark for themselves by skilfully using the internet to promote themselves or their business models. You will find that a great many of them started off fairly young, sometimes in their teens. All of them shared a strong belief in their conviction that they had the right product and service for which there existed a healthy market, and they gave their all in its pursuit.

Not everybody achieves unprecedented growth, but there are many many others who may not count among the world's richest folk, but still have grown exceedingly rich and famous by any standards of the world. Quite honestly, the examples are far too numerous, but what is striking is that most of these individuals began with an original idea at a very young age and made their millions while still under 30 years of age.

Never in the history of mankind, since the advent of civilisation, have so many young people made such prodigious amounts of money at such a young age.

It is the power of the internet which has given wings to the imagination of these new age entrepreneurs and given them the ability to soar. Truly the invention of the internet must rank as highly as the invention of the wheel, the electric bulb and the automobile, in as much that its impact has been epochal.

What is in it for me? What can success on the Internet give you? This is a question which has many parts and you may wonder as to what it is that becoming an internet success would hold of special significance for you? Is it about the money, the fame, the adulation, the popularity, the convergence with likeminded people, or is it about notoriety?

Well, the fact of the matter is that the Internet and internet millionaires are a recent phenomenon and the judgment is yet to be out as to whether it is all good, or whether it is a mixed blessing, and no doubt as the years go by and the golden boys of this era add a few grey hairs to their temples, sociologists and psychologists will write their theses and treatises on the subject but right now it suffices to say that the internet provides unprecedented opportunity, but along with it come the pitfalls, which are really part of the territory if you are looking at a blazing a trail and making a name for yourself.

Consider this. The Internet is a vast ocean of information which you can harness and put to use to further your own objectives. Now, your objective may be something as simple as help in your homework assignment, or you may want to run an online pizza delivery business.

You may even want to write your autobiography and try to make it reach as many people as possible, across the globe. The Internet empowers you to go ahead and accomplish this.

The Internet will let you communicate with whoever you want, anywhere in the world. This means that you can work and be entertained with likeminded people, when you want and where you want, without being at a disadvantage because of your age, sex nationality, religion or geography.

Now, this can be a tremendously liberating thing. You are free to choose who you want to work with, at what time and on what terms. The same applies to recreation and entertainment.

What this means is that the very paradigm of living life as we know it has changed. For the first time in the history of mankind, one has the truest personal freedom of choosing one's career, where you decide your own schedule and give full rein to your creative imagination.

This does not, of course, mean that there is no flip side. Of course there is, just as it is there in everything in life.

There is danger of spamming, identity theft, pornography and vicious virus attacks. But these are illegal activities and you should take all measures to protect yourself against them. If you indulge in such activities yourself, you do so at your own peril as you are breaking the law.

Then there are other pitfalls, not the least among them being Internet addiction. The Internet is a tool that you can use to get ahead in life and also indulge in for some harmless entertainment. If you make it the be all and end all of your life, then you will have no life to talk about.

Your online friends can never fill in for real, physical contact and interaction. Neither can online gaming take the place of a game of basketball. You have got to put things in perspective and you will be alright.

Take the case of Facebook- a great way to socialise and re-establish contact with long lost friends. But you know what? Don't be the fool who lives to update his or her status on it.

Who wants to know what you had for breakfast today? Try using Facebook to launch your business career or for finding employment. It lends itself very nicely to such things, thanks to its vast reach.

The internet can empower you like nothing else, but you've got to be focused on your goals and not get side-tracked by its many distractions. It's like life itself.

The choices you make decide where you go. You can use the Internet to sell your skills and get rich. If fame is your thing, the Internet gives you access to a vast audience, and if you are up to no good and indulge in dirty tricks and sleaze- well, the Internet can provide notoriety too. As they say: to each his own.

Chapter 20

Getting famous online

The Internet can be used to get famous- really famous. There are several ways of doing that. Some have been well documented and in the last chapter we discussed the attributes required to get famous. Given below are five not that well known, very fun, but highly effective ways of getting famous, leveraging the potential of the Internet.

Videos that go viral We come across these supposedly accidentally shot videos of someone doing something remarkable without noticing that they are being filmed. The person may be doing somersaults on the roof of a high rise building practicing his flips right next to a sheer 100 foot drop, oblivious to the danger and enjoying his routine.

Somebody uploads it and the clip has millions of hits online. Soon the man's identity is known and he becomes a household name, and the media are at his door with interview requests, and he is even asked to lecture school kids on the benefits of exercise. Sounds far-fetched, but this is how the phenomenon of viral videos pans out. And mind you these are invariably pre-planned and anything but spontaneous.

Now what is noteworthy here is that a viral video can make you very famous in the proverbial overnight time span, and if you can successfully effect one you have had it made. If one were to learn from the various examples of successful viral videos one will realise that it is not really that difficult to pull it off.

One of the ground rules to follow is that the length has to be kept short in keeping with people's short attention spans and the veritable deluge of viral videos that has descended upon us.

It has to be remembered that a video is not inherently viral. It has to be worked upon and made that way. A whopping 3 billion videos are viewed on YouTube every day!

How do you make yours viral in such a scenario? The content needs to be reached to the right target audience first for it to receive the right push that will make it viral.

To ensure that the video gets the initial attention, it does of course have to create a good first impression. Then the description or transcription that accompanies the video is important too and the key words should be chosen with care.

Remember that YouTube is also a social medium- so get the conversation flowing back and forth by initiating it and actively participating in it. Get the traffic flowing so that it eventually reaches viral proportions.

Go Blog

Blogging is one of the simplest and most effective ways of getting famous, and the best part is that you could be anybody-the average Joe or the wiz-kid of the block; both of you have an equal chance to hit it big by blogging. The basic premise is that there have to be numerous people who are more or less like you and would respond positively and appreciatively to what you put up on your blog.

The way to achieve success is by updating your blog on a regular and consistent basis and by focusing on quality. It might take some time for you to build up your audience, but you will get there if you persevere.

The trick is to socialise. Comment on other people's blogs and get them to comment on yours. Let people know about your blog but do not overdo it. Use the right vehicles like Facebook and Twitter to reach your message to a vast audience in an unobtrusive way.

It might also be a good idea to enable sharing buttons on your website. That apart you can share links with other websites. When you do that, traffic gets diverted from your site to the ones that are linked.

Those sites will get to know of this through a ping back and they may in turn get interested in yours. This way you create a virtuous cycle. Putting together a side-bar embellished with link widgets takes you a step further.

While it is all very well to be blogging regularly you should monitor the direction that your efforts are taking. Find out what constitutes the major portion of your traffic, and customise your posts to cater for that section. It also pays to be a bit smart.

For instance you can closely study the strategy applied by the most successful bloggers and try and replicate it. It might work wonderfully for you and in double quick time too.

Another way of getting noticed by the right people is to occasionally blog as a guest on other sites, which have synergy with your blog. This will put you in direct contact with just the target audience you have always drooled over. This will be your chance to win them over.

In essence blogging is something where time is on your side and you can and will willy nilly make a great success of your blog, if that is what you want to do- really one of the best ways to get famous. The truth of this is borne out by the many success stories of bloggers who have become celebrities in their own right by the very power of their blog posts.

The most famous blog in the world is the Huffington post, which specialises in breaking news pertaining to a wide array of subjects-world news, entertainment, business, politics and fashion. You have traffic; the biggies will be waiting in the wings to pay you a huge some for your coveted blog. That is the way the cookie usually crumbles if you can show substantial traffic to your site.

The point to be noted is the tremendous power of a blog in terms of how famous it can make you and the kind of revenue you can possibly generate. Now not everyone will possibly be this successful, but one can understand that a fair degree of success is possible for anyone who is able to follow the methodologies discussed above.

The degree of success of course depends upon the degree of innovation and capacity to leverage displayed by the individual.

Nothing like Entertaining

If there is anything that people take to instantly, be it the offline world or online world it has to be entertainment. Music, dance, food, fashion and culture make the world go. And if you can put up stuff online that people find genuinely entertaining you are set to achieve success, fame and wealth.

If you are a comedian or a singer or perhaps a painter there is no better way of acquiring a fan base, than being on the Internet. People have this urge to know the smallest detail about famous entertainers-their hobbies, their food habits, their hang out joints and what it is that they wear

If you can get a sizable group of people genuinely interested in your craft, you will have them eating out of your hand, by leveraging such information on the Internet. Get across to your target audience by writing blogs about your performances and posting videos.

Give them a glimpse into your life- your joint performances with other artists, any new deals you may have signed; the works. You have got to remember that your success and livelihood depends upon your fans being happy. So take full advantage of this interactive platform and get to know your fans up close and personally.

Respond to their comments and criticism, chat with them online, send them mails, do everything it takes to keep them hooked on to you and see where that gets you. The thing that is of paramount importance for you should be of identifying the right niche and segment that you want to focus your energies on.

If for example you are excellent at rock ballads but can sing hip hop too, rather than diluting your image by catering to both the segments, it would make sense to focus on your core competency.

You will naturally attract more and better quality traffic with something you are really good at rather than in dabbling in several things you are only average at. In economics this is referred to as the theory of the comparative cost advantage.

Once you are sure of your genre, you have got to give it your all. Use blogging, social media, and YouTube for all its worth and try and form associations everywhere.

A multi-pronged online approach will create opportunities which will sometimes exceed your wildest expectations. A singer might be approached by a multinational record label, and a cookery blogger might get approached by a TV company for their own show.

Notoriety is the flip side of fame. As long as you get the traffic and don't break any laws, you will be attractive to marketers who will want to be a part of the action.

Of course there are also regular entertainers like actors, singers, performing artists, fashion designers and every day people like you and me and not just the weird eccentrics, who use the Internet to entertain, inform and engage! You think you have what it takes to become an entertainer make the Internet your friend. It is cheap, easily accessible and can put you in instant touch with your prospective audience.

Plus you get real time feedback on your performance which you can effectively use to improve your act and make it more in line with what people want. If you get it right, in time you are bound to grow big.

Be a specialist

The Internet is a world that is teeming with people's posts, blogs, articles, pictures, videos, e-books, games and some not so savoury content. How do you get noticed in this bewildering maze of content?

By going back to the economic theory of the advantages of comparative cost and specializing in a particular niche. Now what can that niche be? It is something that you are particularly good at- something that you can call your own.

You are so good and adept at providing that product and service there is no one else who can replace you. The online world is driven by content or information. If you are effectively meeting specific requirements of a set of people better than anyone else, be it in the shape of music that your produce or a game that you create, then for that particular niche you are irreplaceable.

The fact of the matter is that your target audience expects you to be an expert. So you had better be, by doing research and refining your skills. Make it your niche and yours alone and nobody else's.

Once you have the above sorted out and have traffic in place you can go ahead and make money from this traffic. This can be done by signing up for an affiliate program that lets advertisers place their advertisements on your site for a consideration.

Not only do you make money by marketing your own product or service, you also leverage the traffic to your site to earn more money-a win-win situation for you. You can learn from the examples of others who have done wonderfully well for themselves by focusing on the right niche.

Be special

Following up on the above where one talked about creating or discovering one's own niche; this cannot and will not happen unless your product or service is unique and in a class of its own. Before you come to as to what makes you or your offering unique, we need to address a more basic question.

Who are the people that you plan to serve? For example if you plan to be an author, you cannot be writing about everything under the sun and expect to make any headway. There would be so many like you who wouldn't have the slightest clue about what the profile of their average reader would be.

However if you want to be known as an author who writes books whose characters hail from Brisbane, you would be able to identify your target audience-the people of Brisbane. Now you can go all out and woo the people of Brisbane.

How many authors would there be; all of whose characters would be from Brisbane? That would make you unique.

You would be able to, through you books on the city explore different facets of it- its history, its people, its culture, its cuisine, its entertainment hot-spots and so on. You could literally go to town with snippets from your forthcoming books, information about the real life people and events that inspired you, the part of Brisbane you grew up in and other like trivia.

By and by you would create a unique position as the definitive voice on Brisbane. If you are looking for examples of uniqueness saving the day for websites, the successful ones are all unique.

Take the case of Facebook which propounded a unique model of online social networking. Today there may be many copycat sites. But can they replicate even a tiny fraction of the success that accrued to it? Not a chance! Because they were clearly not unique.

Well Facebook may be a legendary example; but there are many many more which validate the contention that being unique is the first step taken towards online celebrity and fame. They naturally have gone to town on the Internet publicising the uniqueness of their products in the most unique way possible.

You may think that this is an over the top and eccentric way to prove that you are unique, but when the stakes are high, can it be otherwise?

Work out your uniqueness quotient before you even begin to think of making mass contact.

That being said, there is nothing in this world that stops you from finding your niche. The Internet universe is a much fairer and more democratic organism than what has ever evolved over the eons, and everybody has a fair chance at communicating with likeminded individuals. This is the Internet's greatest strength. Make it yours

Chapter 21

The Changing Contours of PR

The way that people consume news has completely altered since the advent of social media. From being the main source of news and considered opinion, conventional media comprising of newspapers, magazines, television and radio are now referred to after the news has been consumed online in real time, mostly from social media websites like Facebook and Twitter. The primacy of traditional media is therefore fading right before our eyes.

In the case of India things are a little different in that the growth of literacy accompanied by the growth of purchasing power has seen an explosive growth in vernacular print media. However in so far as the urban centres are concerned online and social media are beginning to rule the roost like elsewhere in the world.

With a gargantuan telecom subscriber base of 1 billion, 220 million of which are smart phone users the reach of online and social media is not to be scoffed at. Internet connectivity as a whole is available to a mammoth 462 million Indians.

However it seems that Indian PR Practitioners are yet to wake up and smell the coffee in that they still deploy most of their resources in chasing journalists representing traditional media. With bottom line pressures buffeting much of the traditional media outlets, objectivity and a professional approach to news inputs is quite often not quite visible. How many traditional journalists care to attend press conferences these days?

Besides even in the case of one- on- ones and interactions there is no guarantee that story will see the light of the day. Rather than continue doing things the old way, PR practitioners should educate their clients about the advantages of online and social PR.

Online news portal journalists and bloggers are generally not only more approachable, but in many cases better able to understand the nuances of the story and are able to render it better. Besides they always reach the right target audience.

The ultimate PR vehicles in my opinion are social media with their enormous reach that can be targeted with infinite precision. There are a whopping 142 million Facebook users in India, 23.2 million Twitter users and 37 million LinkedIn users. The circulation and readership figures of most newspapers and magazines are almost puny in comparison.

The key to leveraging these media lies not in cultivating indifferent and sometimes ignorant journalists, but in the ability to create and post relevant content on behalf of the clients.

This makes the task of the PR practitioners a lot less thankless, and they no longer have to simultaneously contend with capricious clients and journalists. Social Media PR requires the regular creation of germane content, targeted with precision at the right target audience. There are tools that let you post simultaneously and quickly on multiple sites, while others help you give the posts a boost.

The results are quick to come and can be easily tracked and analysed. This kind of outreach is far more dynamic and lets the client interact with their target audience in real-time and in a manner that is personal and intimate.

In comparison the outreach obtained by traditional media is very vague and dispersed and one has no idea how the target audience perceive the message. Online PR is truly the not so distant future.

Chapter 22

The Role of Social Media in PR

The advent of the Internet has been no less revolutionary for the way people relate with the world around them, than the discovery of the use of fire or the invention of wheel was for early man. Among the most important advancements in communication technology that was spawned by the Internet revolution is the introduction of social media channels of communications.

While on the one hand these have diminished the importance of traditional media to communicate on behalf of brands; they have on the other hand provided communicators with a very powerful medium to reach out one's message in quick time to an extremely focused and targeted social media. What's more the effectiveness of the message can be measured on the basis of real time feedback from the recipients.

This has caused a paradigm shift in the way PR or Public Relations professionals have begun to practice outreach on behalf of their clients. The traditional rigmarole of shooting out press releases, holding press conferences, organising interactions and an occasional Op-Ed will no longer do.

In an era where newspapers and TV channels struggle to survive and assorted bloggers, online news portals, and social media messaging redefine the rules of the game all the time; up-skilling is the need of the hour for communication and PR professionals.

The last Indian General Elections saw the now Prime Minister Narendra Modi leverage the power of social media to communicate directly with his target audience-young aspirational India and blow into smithereens the reputation and electoral chances of the more than a century old Congress party which had lorded over the country for more than sixty years. Modi continues to see no use for the cantankerous and noisy traditional media and treats them with the contempt they probably deserve.

No more do you hear of expensive overseas junkets to self-important journalists who think no end of themselves. Instead he would rather engage with the government owned Doordarshan or wires like PTI and ANI.

Above all he continues to rely on social media, which keep him in direct and daily touch with millions of his followers in India and abroad.

There are a number of advantages that accrue to a communications professional, PR consultant or marketer by leveraging the use of social media

1. You can publicly address an issue on an immediate basis:

If a car company has noticed that a lot of complaints have been coming in pertaining to issues with the brakes on a certain model of car, they can immediately address the owners of that particular model on social media, advising them to suspend the use of their car, and wait for the company to contact them for carrying out a rectification of the problem.

This could prevent a crisis in the making and forestall the necessity of an expensive recall across several models.

2. Mass sharing of information:

A company or for that matter a politician can show their concern for their constituency by sending them updates that concern them. A mobile phone manufacturer can let its customers know about upgrades that they can download or new models they can purchase online.

A politician can let the people know of the initiatives they have taken, and what else to expect going forward.

3. Direct and interactive access:

I was once informed about the cancellation of my flight a mere three hours before departure and it took a great deal of effort to somehow get myself a ticket on another airline to make it back home in time. As I wasn't too happy with the way the cancelling airline handled the issue I tweeted about it.

By the time I landed, I had received a response from the airline's customer services department apologising for the inconvenience caused and expressing their desire to speak to me about it and assuage my feelings!

4. Inexpensive:

If you are a self-published author who know that you have a masterpiece on your hands, yet don't have the monetary muscle to publicise your work, get on board the social media marketing and PR express and see how with a relatively small sum of investment you can reach out to hundreds and thousands of prospective buyers.

PR practitioners have to master the art of creating engaging social media posts for their customers. Tools like Hootsuite enable one to post across multiple channels in a manner of minutes, thereby granting the ability to manage the social media campaigns of a large number of clients.

What's more one no longer has to pitch to the mighty mandarins of traditional media hoping that the powers that be see merit in the message you want them to carry. Social Media give you the wherewithal to send out the message that you want without having to worry about journalist oversight.

Any tempering that your content might need will come from your intended target audience and not some self-appointed arbiters of the kind of messaging that is right for your target audience.

Chapter 23

The Best Kind of Content

Everybody agrees that great content is a great idea. The question is what constitutes great content. In the first instance what is content? Is it an amalgamation of written, audio and audio-visual messaging and data? How is content stored?

In documents and audio and video files, some would say. But don't we have content stored in our heads, which we can retrieve as and when we require it?

It follows that content by itself serves no purpose. You may remember all the verses of a holy book, but they would serve no purpose unless you were a priest who needs to recite them at religious ceremonies.

Similarly for a farmer, albeit a modern one, a play by Shakespeare would probably hold little value (unless he is inclined towards the literary arts) while the weather alert he receives on his phone in the shape of text messages would be.

So it would seem that when it comes to creating relevant content, marketers need to follow the horses for courses approach. That being said each type of content has its specific advantages.

1. Written Content: This is the most prolific kind of content that we have known, as man has kept written records of activity since the early days of civilization. All that mankind has learned over thousands of years has been possible with the help of written content. Every subject known to us-history, science, geography, religion and literature was propagated with the help of written content and this continues till today.

Written content gives one the luxury of understanding complex issues and phenomena at length and at a pace that the reader is comfortable with. Besides, this is the cheapest form of communication and provides one with a permanent record for future reference. This is possibly the reason why most official documents in the world are in written form.

2. Audio Content: Audio content has always been in vogue and in fact predates written content. We could hear someone speak, even before we learned to read and write. The modern era saw radio being put to great use by leaders to broadcast their message simultaneously to vast multitudes of people, something not possible prior to that.

Politicians and entertainers were quick to grasp the potential of this new medium of communication and used it with telling effect for propaganda and publicity. Then of course there is the advantage of being better able to communicate with the visually impaired and those with poor education.

That apart it is a pretty efficient and cost effective means of quickly communicating with large masses of people Telemarketers who are trained to pitch skilfully on the telephone are a great example of audio content being put to efficient use. Of course with the advent of the Internet and chatting software audio content can be transmitted seamlessly across the world.

3. Audio Visual Content: In terms of receptivity and retention, this is definitely the most impactful means of communication. That is possibly the reason why Shakespeare's plays, which were essentially meant to be an audio visual form of communication courtesy the medium of theatre, became so universally popular.

The advent of cinema showed how truly powerful this medium was with masses of people literally hero worshipping the actors and actresses who essayed myriad parts on the silver-screen. Television further extended the reach of the audio visual format and today with the advent of social media and the Internet, it has assumed a life of its own with anybody being able to create and promote it.

Audio video content has grown in importance tremendously because of the technology aided ease of creation and this has led to it being the flavour of the season for all kind of marketing. Audio video content or video content has inherent advantages that makes it a more potent tool than any other form of communication.

Firstly video content comes closest in simulating real life situations and is therefore able to immediately connect with the audience on a more emotional level than any other form of content. Moreover it closely approximates word of mouth advocacy which is statistically the best way of promoting anything. This is the reason why social video campaigns generate billions of views worldwide.

If people are really taken in by a video, they tend to share it and that is what explains its popularity. That is why more and more companies are embedding videos on their websites. Who knows that their content may go viral and bring them millions of customers?!

Chapter 24

The Internet of Things, Artificial Intelligence and Robotics

Nothing is going to change the way we live our lives more than the Internet of Things, Artificial Intelligence and Robotics. While these technologies will make life a lot easier and businesses more efficient and profitable there is a huge flip side as well.

This has to do with dwindling employment prospects and if some prominent scientists are to be believed, artificially intelligent machines might one day turn on their creators and destroy all humanity! The Internet of things is expected to connect people, data, processes and devices on a gargantuan scale by the end of the decade-a whopping 50 billion connections.

Before one starts worrying about the prospects of humanity being at risk from a take-over by machines, one needs to figure out how the opportunities presented by the Internet of Things are put to optimal use, which in itself will require some doing.

The biggest existential threat to us will not be from sci-fi movie like scenarios where artificially intelligent machines and robots will rebel against humans, but by the security vulnerability that this

Mass-scale convergence could lead to. A less than perfectly designed system could for example impact upon the whole network and lead to disastrous consequences on an unprecedented scale.

Considering that real artificial intelligence is presently at an infantile stage, it is rather silly to be tilting at wind-mills when we worry about the danger it poses to humans. Let us learn to fully reap the benefits that the Internet of things, some rudimentary artificial intelligence and smartly evolving robotic technologies bring to us.

When the time comes, we will ourselves find the solution to any potential threat in the future. We always have. In the meantime we need to prepare our youngsters to handle these emerging technologies as this will help them find employment in the times ahead.

There will of course be job losses for some on account of the increase in all round automation, but there will be other opportunities aplenty for those who anticipate and prepare for the paradigm shift in the way businesses and organisation will conduct their affairs in the times ahead. We are entering very interesting times indeed.

Other books by Vipin Labroo

The Car Driver

A tale of friendship, travel, self-discovery, spirituality and mysticism against the backdrop of mighty Himalayan vistas. Partly travelogue, partly adventure and partly mystery, all the parts come together to render an uplifting tale of redemption

Rambling Musings and a Few Short Stories

This book is a compilation of blogs that I have written on stray issues which caught my fancy as well as a few essays and short stories over the period of the last three years. In a sense they are a reflection of life as seen through the eyes of an urban middle class Indian professional who has witnessed his country transforming rapidly from a laid back and sluggish giant into a throbbing engine of world economic growth that swears by consumerism even as he went about his mundane daily life.

Live the Internet Life

The Internet has afforded an incredible opportunity to talented youngsters to grow their business in an unprecedented manner. This lets them lead the fabulous Internet Life